Contents

C000152407

Equipment
For general cake decorating
You will find the following list of general equipment useful when decorating cakes and cookies.

1 Cake boards
 Drum – 12mm (½in) thick board to display cakes
 Hardboard – a thin strong board, usually the same size as the cake, which is placed under cake to act as a barrier and to give stability to stacked cakes

2 Carving knife – a sharp long-bladed pastry knife, for levelling cakes and carving shapes

3 Cocktail sticks (toothpicks) – used as markers and to transfer small amounts of edible paste colour

4 Dowels – used in conjunction with hardboards to support tiered cakes

5 Measuring spoons – for accurate measurement of ingredients

6 Paintbrushes – a range of sizes is useful for stippling, painting and dusting

7 Paint palette – for mixing edible paste colours and dusts prior to painting and dusting

8 Rolling pin – for rolling out the different types of paste

9 Scissors – for cutting templates and trimming paste to shape

10 Set square – for accurate alignment

11 Spacers – 1.5mm (¹⁄₁₆in) and 5mm (³⁄₁₆in) for rolling out paste

12 Spirit level – to check dowels are vertical and tops of cakes are horizontal

13 Tins (pans) – for baking cakes ball, round and multi-sized

14 Non-stick work board – for rolling out pastes

15 Smoother – to give a smooth and even finish to sugarpaste

16 Sugar shaper and discs – to create pieces of uniformly shaped modelling paste

17 Modelling tools
 Ball tool (FMM) – gives even indentations in paste and softens the edges of petals
 Craft knife – for intricate cutting tasks
 Cutting wheel (PME) – use instead of a knife to avoid dragging the paste
 Dresden tool – to create markings on paste
 Palette knife – for cutting paste and spreading royal icing
 Quilting tool (PME) – for adding stitching lines
 Scriber (PME) – for scribing around templates, popping air bubbles in paste and removing small sections of paste

Stencils

For the best and most satisfying results on your cakes, I recommend you use laser-cut culinary stencils made from durable food-grade plastic, as shown here.

There is a huge selection of culinary stencils available, so choosing a design can sometimes be a little tricky. The first consideration is the scale of the item you wish to decorate. You will need a much smaller-scale pattern for stencilling a cookie or cupcake than for a cake board. However, using part of a larger pattern on a cupcake or cookie can work very effectively, and repeating a small-scale pattern around the edge of a cake board is often very successful.

Sugar Recipes

Most of the sugar recipes used in this booklet for covering and decoration can easily be made at home. Use edible paste colours to colour them according to the individual project.

Sugarpaste (rolled fondant)

Used to cover cakes and boards, ready-made sugarpaste can be obtained from major supermarkets and cake-decorating suppliers, and is available in white and the whole colour spectrum. It is also easy and inexpensive to make your own.

Ingredients
Makes 1kg (2¼lb)

★ 60ml (4 tbsp) cold water
★ 20ml (4 tsp/1 sachet) powdered gelatine
★ 125ml (4 fl oz) liquid glucose
★ 15ml (1 tbsp) glycerine
★ 1kg (2¼lb) icing (confectioners') sugar, sifted, plus extra for dusting

tip...

For tips and discussion about making your own sugarpaste, visit the Lindy's Cakes blog.

1 Place the water in a small bowl, sprinkle over the gelatine and soak until spongy. Stand the bowl over a saucepan of hot but not boiling water and stir until the gelatine is dissolved. Add the glucose and glycerine, stirring until well blended and runny.

2 Put the sifted icing (confectioners') sugar in a large bowl. Make a well in the centre and slowly pour in the liquid ingredients, stirring constantly. Mix well.

3 Turn out onto a surface dusted with icing (confectioners') sugar and knead until smooth, sprinkling with extra sugar if the paste becomes too sticky. The paste can be used immediately or tightly wrapped and stored in a plastic bag until required.

Modelling paste

Used to add decoration to cakes, this versatile paste keeps its shape well and dries harder than sugarpaste. Although there are commercial pastes available, it is easy and a lot cheaper to make your own – I always do!

Ingredients
Makes 225g (8oz)

★ 225g (8oz) sugarpaste (rolled fondant)
★ 5ml (1 tsp) gum tragacanth

Make a well in the sugarpaste and add the gum tragacanth. Knead in. Wrap in a plastic bag and allow the gum to work before use. You will begin to feel a difference in the paste after an hour or so, but it is best left overnight. The modelling paste should be firm but pliable with a slight elastic texture. Kneading the modelling paste makes it warm and easy to work with.

Modelling paste tips
★ Gum tragacanth is a natural gum available from cake-decorating suppliers.
★ If time is short use CMC (Tylose) instead of gum tragacanth – this a synthetic alternative but it works almost straight away.
★ Placing your modelling paste in a microwave for a few seconds is an excellent way of warming it for use.
★ If you have previously added a large amount of colour to your paste and it is consequently too soft, an extra pinch or two of gum tragacanth will be necessary.
★ If your paste is crumbly or too hard to work, add a touch of white vegetable fat (shortening) and a little cooled boiled water and knead until softened.

White vegetable fat (shortening)

This is a solid white vegetable fat (shortening) that is often known by a brand name: in the UK, Trex or White Flora; in South Africa, Holsum; in Australia, Copha; and in America, Crisco. These products are more or less interchangeable in cake making.

Royal icing

Royal icing is used in several of the projects in this booklet, and below are recipes for two methods for making it.

Quick royal icing

This is a very quick method, which is ideal if time is short or you just wish use a stencil.

Ingredients
- ★ 1 large (US extra large) egg white
- ★ 250g (9oz) icing (confectioners') sugar, sifted

Put the egg white in a bowl, lightly beat to break it down then gradually beat in the icing sugar until the icing is glossy and forms soft peaks.

Professional royal icing

This is a more involved method that gives you a better quality of icing, ideal for finer details. Make sure all your equipment is spotless, as even small residues of grease will affect the icing.

Ingredients
- ★ 90g (3oz) egg white (approx 3 eggs or equivalent of dried albumen)
- ★ 455g (1lb) icing (confectioners') sugar, sifted
- ★ 5–7 drops of lemon juice (if using fresh eggs)

1 Separate the egg whites the day before needed, sieve through a fine sieve or tea strainer, cover and then place in a refrigerator to allow the egg white to strengthen.

2 Place the egg whites into the bowl of a mixer, stir in the icing (confectioners') sugar and add the lemon juice.

3 Using the whisk attachment, beat as slowly as possible for between 10 and 20 minutes until the icing reaches soft peaks. How long it takes will depend on your mixer. Take care not to over mix – test by lifting a little icing out of the bowl. If the icing forms a peak that bends over slightly, it is the correct consistency.

4 Store in an airtight container, cover the top surface with cling film (plastic wrap) and then a clean damp cloth to prevent the icing forming a crust, before adding the lid and placing in a refrigerator.

Royal icing tips
- ★ The secret to using royal icing on stencils is to make your icing the correct consistency. You should aim to have a reasonably stiff soft peak icing that will not seep under the stencil or flood the stencilled pattern once the stencil is removed.
- ★ To adjust the consistency, either add icing (confectioners') sugar to thicken it, or cooled boiled water to soften it.
- ★ Experiment on a spare piece of sugarpaste before you stencil directly onto a cake or board.
- ★ You will find that some stencil patterns are more forgiving than others, but generally the finer and closer the detail, the stiffer the icing must be to achieve a really good result.

Sugar glue

You can often just use water to stick your sugar decorations to your cakes, however if you find you need something a little stronger try using sugar glue, which is a quick, easy, instant glue to make.

Break up pieces of white modelling paste into a small container and cover with boiling water. Stir until dissolved or to speed up the process place in a microwave for 10 seconds before stirring. This produces a thick strong glue, which can be easily thinned by adding some more cooled boiled water.

Piping gel

Piping gel is a multi-purpose transparent gel that is excellent for attaching sugarpaste to cookies. It also can add shimmering accents and colourful highlights. It is available commercially but is just as easy to make.

Ingredients
- ★ 30ml (2 tbsp) powdered gelatine
- ★ 30ml (2 tbsp) cold water
- ★ 500ml (18 fl oz) golden syrup (corn syrup)

Sprinkle the gelatine over the cold water in a small saucepan and leave to set for about five minutes. Heat on low until the gelatine has become clear and dissolved – do not boil. Add the syrup and stir thoroughly. Cool and store, refrigerated, for up to two months.

Silver Swirls

STENCILLING ON COOKIES USING
EDIBLE METALLIC LUSTRE DUST

These glamorous cookies
were created using edible
metallic dust, which gives
a very contemporary feel.

You will need

- ★ Heart cookies and
  cutter (W nesting
  hearts)

- ★ Sugarpaste: pink

- ★ Snowflake edible
  lustre dust (SK)

- ★ Contemporary
  valentine heart
  cookie top stencil
  set (DS)

- ★ White vegetable fat
  (shortening)

- ★ Piping gel

- ★ Basic equipment
  (see pages 2–3)

tip...
*Use a soft brush to
achieve a uniform finish
– if the bristles are too
firm they may leave
marks on the surface.*

1 Roll out the sugarpaste to a thickness of
5mm (³⁄₁₆in), ideally using spacers. Place the
stencil on top of the sugarpaste. To ensure
clean, sharp edges, place a smoother on top
of the stencil and press down firmly so that the
sugarpaste is forced up to the upper surface
of the stencil.

2 Next, smear a thin layer of white vegetable
fat (shortening) over the surface of the
sugarpaste pattern i.e. the paste that has been
forced up through the stencil. Use either a
finger or a suitable paintbrush to do this.

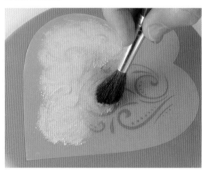

3 Take a large, soft dusting brush and dip
it into the edible lustre dust, knock off any
excess then liberally dust over the stencil,
adding more dust as needed. Brush off any
excess dust from the stencil – this ensures
that as you lift the stencil no stray dust falls
from it, spoiling the pattern beneath. Use
the brush to burnish the dust (if the product
allows) to make it really shine.

4 Carefully lift the stencil away from the paste
to reveal the pattern. You may need to use two
hands to do this.

5 Cut out a shape using the same cutter that
you used to make the cookie. Remove the
excess paste from around the shape. Then,
using a cranked handled palette knife and
a quick swipe action so as not to distort the
shape, position the knife under the sugarpaste.

6 Carefully lift the stencilled sugarpaste shape
and position it onto a cookie that has been
covered with piping gel. Remove the palette
knife and if necessary, using a clean finger,
press the paste so it is all in contact with the
cookie. If you need to do this more than once,
ensure that your fingers are clean, as you do
not want to spoil the pattern.

Using Edible Dusts

When using dusts to stencil your cakes and cookies, it is very important
to ensure that the products you are using are edible. Read the small
print on the pots of dusts that you have to make sure that the ones you
are using are not for decoration purposes only. If they are edible they
will have an ingredients list and a best before date.

Love Hearts

STENCILLING ON CUPCAKES USING
EDIBLE MATT DUSTS

Matt dusts were used to
create this soft, romantic
design on a cupcake.

You will need

- ★ Cupcakes baked in
  purple paper cases

- ★ Sugarpaste: white

- ★ Edible dust colours:
  rose (SK), superwhite
  (SF)

- ★ Holiday cookie tops
  stencil (DS)

- ★ Round pastry
  cutter, same size as
  cupcakes

- ★ Basic equipment
  (see pages 2–3)

1 Roll out the sugarpaste to a thickness of
5mm (³⁄₁₆in), ideally using spacers. Place
your stencil on top of the sugarpaste. Using
a smoother, gently press onto the stencil just
enough to prevent it moving.

2 Mix edible dust colours to create a suitable
shade – I have used a dark pink and white
to create a mid-pink. Dip your brush into the
dust, knock off any excess then carefully dust
over the stencil. Vary the intensity of colour by
adding more or less dust to various sections
of the pattern as desired. Brush off any excess
dust from the stencil – this ensures that as
you lift the stencil no stray dust falls from it,
spoiling the pattern beneath.

3 Carefully lift the stencil to reveal the pattern.
Cut out a circle from the stencilled sugarpaste
to fit the top of your cupcake then gently lift it
and position onto a cupcake using a palette
knife. If necessary, press the paste with a clean
finger so it is all in contact with the cupcake.
Make sure you use a clean finger each time
you do this, so that you don't spoil the pattern.

Perfect Peonies

STENCILLING ON CUPCAKES USING EDIBLE MULTICOLOUR MATT DUSTS

A range of different coloured matt dusts were used to create this stunning cupcake design.

You will need

★ Cupcakes baked in purple paper cases

★ Sugarpaste: white

★ Edible dusts: pink, purple, green, white

★ Peony cake top stencil (LC)

★ Round pastry cutter, same size as cupcakes

★ Basic equipment (see pages 2–3)

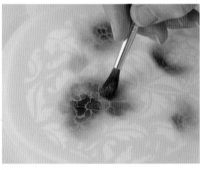

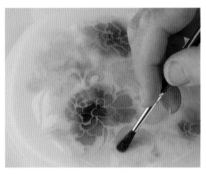

1 Roll out the sugarpaste as for Love Hearts (see page 8) then place your stencil on top of the sugarpaste. Mix different dusts to create suitable colours. Dip a soft brush into one of the dusts, knock off any excess then carefully dust over sections of the stencil, varying the intensity of colour by adding more or less dust. For example, dust the centre of the flower with dark purple then add a light dusting to some of the petals and the edges of leaves.

2 Take a clean brush, dip it into another colour and carefully dust over new sections of the pattern. For example, add some light pink to the outer petals of the flower. Add as many colours to your stencil as you wish, but try to use clean brushes when changing colour and remove all excess dust between colours to ensure that they do not become muddy.

3 Carefully lift the stencil away from the paste to reveal the pattern. Add to the cupcake, as described in step 3 of Love Hearts (see page 8).

Wonky Wedding

STENCILLING ON COOKIES USING ROYAL ICING

Royal icing was used to stencil designs on the 'tiers' of this wonky cake cookie. There is scope to decorate with an endless variety of colours and designs, so don't be afraid to experiment and create something unique.

You will need

★ Wonky wedding cake cookies and cutter (LC)

★ Sugarpaste: deep purple, claret, lilac

★ Royal icing: lilac, tint of pink, purple

★ Stencils: winterthur heart set (DS), chinese floral circle (LC)

★ Basic equipment (see pages 2–3)

1 Roll out the sugarpaste to a thickness of 5mm (³⁄₁₆in). Cut out the shape using the cookie cutter, but leave the surrounding paste in place so that the stencil lies flat. Place the stencil on top and use a palette knife to spread royal icing carefully over the relevant section. Use one or two strokes going from side to side. Do not lift the knife as this may move the stencil and smudge the pattern.

2 Once the icing is of an even thickness, carefully remove the stencil. The thickness of the royal icing is very much personal preference. If it is applied thinly then interesting two-tone effects can be created where the sugarpaste colour is visible through the icing. If the icing is applied more thickly then the pattern has a more three-dimensional textured effect.

3 Using a palette knife, if required, cut the stencilled paste to the required shape. For this example, cut the lower tier of the wonky cake from the upper tiers. Remove all the excess sugarpaste from around the stencilled shape. Paint piping gel over the cookie to act as glue.

4 Using a clean palette knife and a quick swipe action so as not to distort the shape, position the knife under the sugarpaste before carefully lifting the shape and placing it on top of the cookie. Repeat using other colours of sugarpaste and royal icing, choosing colour combinations and stencil patterns that complement each other.

tip...
To clean your stencils, place them in a bowl of water to dissolve the royal icing and then pat them dry.

Tea at the Ritz

STENCILLING ON CUPCAKES USING ROYAL ICING

Using white royal icing on a coloured background creates a stylish cupcake, set off by metallic high tea cupcake cases.

You will need

★ Cupcakes baked in black and silver metallic high tea cases

★ Sugarpaste: red with a touch of pink

★ Royal icing

★ Superwhite dust (SF)

★ Winterthur heart stencil set (DS)

★ Round pastry cutter, same size as cupcakes

★ Basic equipment (see pages 2–3)

1 Roll out the sugarpaste to a thickness of 5mm (³⁄₁₆in). Cut out a circle to fit the top of your cupcake, but leave the surrounding paste in place so that the stencil lies flat. Place the stencil on top and use a palette knife to spread royal icing over the relevant section. Use one or two strokes going from side to side. Do not lift the knife as this may cause the stencil to lift and smudge the pattern.

2 Once the royal icing is of an even thickness, remove the stencil and carefully peel away the excess sugarpaste.

3 Using a cranked handled palette knife and a quick swipe action, position the knife under the sugarpaste circle and carefully lift and place it on top of the cupcake. Leave for a few minutes to allow the royal icing to dry – try to avoid the temptation to touch it.

4 The sugarpaste circle should more or less have fallen into place, however it may be necessary to press down the edges of the circle gently so they are in full contact with the cupcake. Doing this once the royal icing has dried prevents the pattern being distorted or smudged.

tip...
If using white royal icing, add a little superwhite dust to give an opaque rather than a translucent finish.

Pretty in Pink

STENCILLING ON CAKES
USING ROYAL ICING

Royal icing just a few shades darker than the sugarpaste was used to subtly decorate this pretty peony cake.

You will need

★ 12.5cm (5in) round cake

★ 20cm (8in) round cake drum

★ Sugarpaste: 500g (1lb 2oz) each pink, very pale pink

★ Royal icing

★ Pink edible paste colour

★ Stencils: peony cake top design (LC), peony cake side design (LC)

★ Stencil side fixing kit

★ 15mm (½in) wide dusky pink ribbon

★ Pink sugar peony (full instructions on how to make this can be found in *The Contemporary Cake Decorating Bible – Flowers* booklet)

★ Basic equipment (see pages 2–3)

1 Separately cover the cake and cake drum with the very pale pink and pink sugarpaste (see page 26). When covering your cake, ensure that the sides of your cake are vertical using a set square then allow the icing to set.

The tops of the board and cake

2 Colour some royal icing to complement your colour scheme using edible paste or liquid colours. Place your chosen stencil centrally on the covered cake or board, then place your icing in the centre of the stencil so the weight of the icing acts as an anchor, preventing the stencil from moving.

3 Using either a cranked handled palette knife or the longer straight edge of a side scraper, carefully begin spreading the icing out from the centre using radial strokes that go right to the edge of the stencil. Remove any excess icing that remains on your knife or scraper at the end of each stroke.

4 Once the stencil is completely covered, work towards achieving an even thickness of icing, removing any excess with more careful strokes. Once you are happy with the finish, peel away the stencil carefully.

tip...
A slight error in a royal iced stencilled pattern can be corrected with a damp paintbrush while the icing is still wet.

On the side of the cake

5 Use a stencil side fixing kit to secure the stencil in place. You might also find it helpful to insert a couple of pins at one end of the stencil to prevent movement.

6 Take a side scraper and load it with royal icing then, starting at the end of the stencil secured with pins, carefully begin spreading the icing along the stencil. Add more icing as necessary, ensuring that the pattern is completely covered. Try to achieve an even thickness of icing, removing any excess with careful strokes.

7 Once you are happy with the finish, carefully remove the pins and undo the fixing kit to reveal the pattern. If you wish to add another section of stencil design, allow the royal icing to dry before repeating the process. Place the sugar peony on the top of the cake to complete your cake design.

tip...

Practise this technique on a cake dummy or cake tin before you try it on an actual cake.

Geisha Girls

STENCILLING MULTICOLOUR
EFFECTS ON CUPCAKES USING
ROYAL ICING

Exciting multicolour effects
can be created using
different colours of royal
icing on one stencil. This
Japanese-inspired design
was stencilled using
different shades of pink
icing from very pale to
very bold.

You will need

- ★ Cupcakes baked
  in deep pink paper
  cases

- ★ Sugarpaste: pink
  with a touch of red

- ★ Royal icing: white
  (whitened with
  superwhite dust)
  (SF), dark pink, pink

- ★ Japanese flower and
  scroll pattern stencils
  (LC)

- ★ Round pastry
  cutter, same size as
  cupcakes

- ★ Basic equipment
  (see pages 2–3)

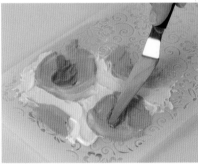

1 Separately colour small amounts of royal
icing, using superwhite dust to whiten, if
necessary, and edible paste or liquid colours
to colour. Lay your stencil over your rolled-
out sugarpaste then add dollops of different
colours to different sections of the stencil,
ideally using different palette knives for speed.

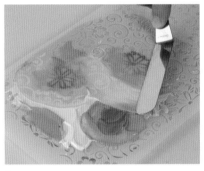

2 Take a clean palette knife and, using a few
careful strokes, spread and merge the colours
of the royal icing. The way in which you do this
will determine how the colours are distributed
over the stencil, so carefully consider the
effect that you are aiming for before you start
spreading the icing.

3 Once you are happy with the effect and the
icing is of an even thickness, carefully remove
the stencil. If you wish to decorate a whole
batch of cupcakes, for example, allow enough
royal icing of each colour – you can reuse the
excess icing you remove from each stencil but
your colours may not be as distinct.

4 When the icing is dry, cut out circles of
the appropriate size and place on top of the
cupcakes (see page 30).

Designer Daisies

ADDING CUT-OUT EMBELLISHMENTS
TO STENCILLED COOKIES

Beautifully stencilled
cookies can be
embellished to your heart's
content. To create this cute
cookie design, a scroll
stencil has been used
together with cut outs.

1 Stencil the design onto the black sugarpaste
with the pink royal icing (see page 10) and
place on top of the cookie (see page 30).

You will need

★ Swimming costume
cookies and cutter (LC)

★ Sugarpaste: black, red

★ Modelling paste: red,
pink, black

★ Pink royal icing

★ Flower scroll stencil (DS)

★ Daisy marguerite cutters
(PME)

★ Piping tubes (tips): PME
no. 16, 17

★ Basic equipment (see
pages 2–3)

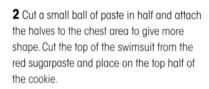

2 Cut a small ball of paste in half and attach
the halves to the chest area to give more
shape. Cut the top of the swimsuit from the
red sugarpaste and place on the top half of
the cookie.

3 Use a plunger cutter to embellish the design
with cut-out daisies. Choose your colours
carefully and think about scale – you want to
create the illusion that the pattern and cut out
are one.

Other Embellishment Methods

Piping Try adding piped royal
icing dots in either the same,
a tonal or a contrasting colour.
These can be piped on top of the
stencilled pattern to great effect. Try
experimenting to see how you can
change the look and impact of a
stencilled pattern with piped dots.

Moulds Using a moulded embellishment made from one of
the thousands of food-grade silicon moulds now available
is a fast and effective way to add more colour and interest
to your stencilled pattern. Try experimenting with moulded
shapes or flowers to see what works with your design.

Tiers of Joy

MAKING YOUR OWN STENCILS
USING READILY AVAILABLE
MATERIALS

Don't be limited by the range of commercial stencils when you can make your own. For this attractive cookie project a craft knife and paper punch have been used to create the stencils, but try experimenting with other materials that you may have to hand.

You will need

* Wedding cake cookies and cutter (LC)

* Sugarpaste: pink with a touch of red, white

* Royal icing

* Superwhite dust (SF)

* Card or waxed paper

* Craft knife

* Paper punch

* Edible dust colours

* Basic equipment (see pages 2–3)

1 To make stencils for the top and bottom tiers: Draw or transfer your design – here I have drawn with a pencil onto card, however you could easily trace an appropriate image or logo. Place the card onto a cutting mat or suitable surface and use a craft knife to cut away sections of the design to create the stencil.

2 To make stencils for the middle tier: Use a general craft punch with a daisy design for this. Note that not all punches will cut through card, so you may need to use another material such as waxed paper, which is not as durable.

3 Stencil your designs onto the sugarpastes with whitened royal icing and edible dusts (see page 10) then place on top of the different tiers of the cookie (see page 30).

tip...
General craft punches work really well if you want a design near the edge of your stencil.

Logolicious!

MAKING YOUR OWN STENCILS USING SPECIALIST TOOLS

The Lindy's Cakes logo motif on the cupcake in this contemporary project was cut from a plastic stencil sheet with a heat tool.

You will need

- ★ Cupcakes baked in deep pink paper cases

- ★ Sugarpaste: purple

- ★ White vegetable fat (shortening)

- ★ Stencil tool

- ★ Plastic stencil sheet

- ★ Edible lustre dust

- ★ Round pastry cutter, same size as cupcakes

- ★ Basic equipment (see pages 2–3)

1 Place your design under your plastic stencil sheet and secure with tape. Heat up the stencil tool – this usually takes about five minutes. The tip of the tool gets extremely hot so be very careful to prevent any accidental burning. Always read and follow the manufacturer's instructions carefully.

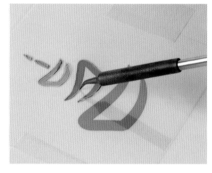

2 Hold the tool in your hand so the nib is vertical and your hand is resting on your work surface, as if you were writing. Trace around your design quickly and smoothly, applying just enough pressure to feel the surface below the tip (the cut is made with heat, not pressure). Try not to linger at any point, as continuous heat could damage the stencil.

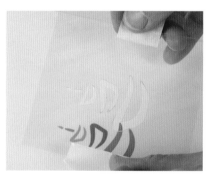

3 Once you are happy with your design, stencil it onto the purple sugarpaste using the edible lustre dust, as shown on page 6. To add interest, if desired, press lightly around the stencilled pattern with a cutter or stick embosser. Cut out a circle of paste and place on top of the cupcake (see page 30).

tip...

As with any technique, you'll find that you improve with practice so try out the tool on small designs first before embarking on a larger project.

Funky Flip Flops

USING STENCILS TO EMBOSS
SUGARPASTE DESIGNS ON
COOKIES

These fun flip flop cookies
have been embossed
using a stencil to leave a
distinctive raised pattern
on the soles.

You will need

★ Flip flop cookies and
   cutter (LC)

★ Sugarpaste: deep
   pink

★ Modelling paste:
   purple, white, light
   pink

★ Greek repeat pattern
   stencil (LC)

★ Mini flower mould (FI
   – FL107)

★ Basic equipment
   (see pages 2–3)

1 Roll out the deep pink sugarpaste to
a thickness of 5mm (³⁄₁₆in), ideally using
spacers. Place your stencil on top of the
paste. Using a smoother, press down firmly so
that the sugarpaste is forced up to the upper
surface of the stencil. Repeat for the remainder
of the pattern.

2 Carefully remove the stencil and, if required,
reposition and repeat. Then cut out the shapes
with your chosen cutters and place on the top
of the cookies (see page 30).

3 To make the straps, cut 1cm (³⁄₈in) wide
strips of purple modelling paste and mitre one
end of each. Take a mitred end and attach
about halfway down the foot. Twist the strip
180 degrees towards the centre of the shoe,
position the twisted strip so the strap finishes
between the toes and cut off the excess paste.
Repeat for second strap and add a two-colour
moulded modelling paste flower to cover
the join.

tip...
*I find using stencils for embossing particularly useful if I want
to add a subtle pattern to a large area such as a cake board.*

Stacked Hatboxes

YOUR STENCILLED MASTERPIECE!

The beautiful, intricate patterns on these boxes are created simply using culinary stencils, royal icing and edible dusts, as demonstrated throughout this booklet.

You will need

- ★ Round cakes: 25.5cm (10in), 20cm (8in), 15cm (6in)

- ★ Round hardboard cake boards: 25.5cm (10in), 20cm (8in), 15cm (6in)

- ★ 35cm (14in) round cake drum

- ★ Sugarpaste: 1.6kg (3½lb) each very pale pink (board, top tier), purple (bottom tier); 500g (1lb 2oz) each pale pink (middle tier), claret (middle tier)

- ★ Modelling paste: 225g (8oz) pale pink, 175g (6oz) very pale pink, 50g (2oz) each purple, claret

- ★ Edible dust colours: pink (rose SK), claret (cyclamen SK), purple (violet SK), pastel pink and superwhite (SF)

- ★ Royal icing

- ★ Stencils: damask cake side design (DS), leafy scroll side design (DS), chic rose side design (DS), chic rose circle design (DS)

- ★ Stencil side fixing kit

- ★ Multi-sized ribbon cutter (FMM)

- ★ Sugar shaper

- ★ 15mm (½in) wide claret ribbon

- ★ Two sugar peonies with two sets of leaves each (full instructions on how to make these can be found in *The Contemporary Cake Decorating Bible – Flowers* booklet)

- ★ Basic equipment (see pages 2–3)

1 Cover the cake drum with 800g (1¾lb) pale pink sugarpaste (see page 29) and emboss using the rose circle design and a smoother (see page 21). Trim to fit.

2 Place each cake on the appropriate hardboard cake board and cover in two sections as shown on page 28, covering the sides before the top. This ensures a sharp edge to the top of the cake and that the join is later covered by the rim of the lid.

3 For the bottom tier: Either raise the cake up or turn the cake upside down and position the stencil so that the pattern starts at the base of the cake, using a side fixing kit. Stencil the side design using royal icing whitened with superwhite dust and tinted with claret dust colour (see page 16). Repeat and mask as necessary (see box overleaf).

tip...
To clean your stencils, place them in a bowl of water to dissolve the royal icing and then pat them dry.

Adjusting a Stencil to Fit

You will often find that your chosen stencil design is not quite the right size or shape for your cake. If so, adjust it to fit using pattern repeat or masking techniques, which can be used separately or together as necessary.

Pattern Repeat This is particularly useful when stencilling the side of a cake and most side stencils are designed in such a way that any join in the pattern looks seamless. The secret is to allow the first pattern to dry and to wash and dry the stencil before attempting the repeat. When ready, position the stencil so that the pattern looks continuous and apply royal icing as previously described.

Masking This may be necessary when using pattern repeats around a cake to ensure that you have a perfect fit. It is also necessary when you wish to use only part of a stencil design. To mask a stencil, simply cover the areas of the design around the section you wish to use with masking tape. This allows you to spread the icing without accidentally stencilling more of the pattern than you intended.

tip...
Clean, dry and store your stencils carefully to ensure
that they stay in tip-top condition.

4 For the middle tier: Using narrow spacers, roll out the pale pink modelling paste into a long strip large enough to fit around the cake. Stencil the strip using the leafy scroll stencil and edible dusts (see page 8). Cut one long edge straight. Paint sugar glue over the side of the cake and carefully, with the help of an extra pair of hands if possible, transfer your stencilled paste to the cake.

8 Dowel and stack the cakes and place on the board, leaving room for the peony. Take the two peonies and four sets of leaves and position on the cake and board to complete.

5 For the top tier: Use a modelling paste strip as for the middle tier but use royal icing to stencil the design (see page 14).

6 Add appropriately coloured lid rims to all the hatboxes by rolling sugarpaste into long sausages and then rolling the paste out to an even 5mm (³⁄₁₆in) thickness. Cut strips using a multi-sized ribbon cutter and attach (see page 29).

7 Neaten the top edge of each cake using modelling paste and a sugar shaper fitted with the medium ribbon disc. Add modelling paste ribbons, cut with a multi-sized ribbon cutter, as desired (see page 29).

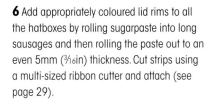

tip...
A slight error in a royal iced stencilled pattern can be corrected with a damp paintbrush while the icing is still wet.

Covering Cakes and Boards

Follow these techniques to achieve a neat and professional appearance to your cakes, cupcakes, cookies and cake boards. With care and practice, you will soon find that you have a perfectly smooth finish.

Levelling the cake

Making an accurate cake base is an important part of creating your masterpiece. There are two ways to do this, depending on the cake:

Method 1 Place a set square up against the edge of the cake and, with a sharp knife, mark a line around the top of the cake at the required height: 7–7.5cm (2¾–3in). With a large serrated knife cut around the marked line and across the cake to remove the domed crust.

Method 2 Place a cake board into the base of the tin (pan) in which the cake was baked so that when the cake is placed on top, the outer edge of the cake will be level with the tin, and the dome will protrude above. Take a long, sharp knife and cut the dome from the cake, keeping the knife against the tin. This will ensure the cake is completely level.

Sugarpaste quantities

Cake sizes		Sugarpaste quantities – 5mm (³⁄₁₆in) thickness
Round	Square	
7.5cm (3in)		275g (10oz)
10cm (4in)	7.5cm (3in)	350g (12oz)
12.5cm (5in)	10cm (4in)	425g (15oz)
15cm (6in)	12.5cm (5in)	500g (1lb 2oz)
18cm (7in)	15cm (6in)	750g (1lb 10oz)
20cm (8in)	18cm (7in)	900g (2lb)
23cm (9in)	20cm (8in)	1kg (2¼lb)
25.5cm (10in)	23cm (9in)	1.25kg (2¾lb)
28cm (11in)	25.5cm (10in)	1.5kg (3lb)
30cm (12in)	28cm (11in)	1.75kg (3¾lb)
33cm (13in)	30cm (12in)	2kg (4½lb)
35.5cm (14in)	33cm (13in)	2.25kg (4lb 15oz)

Note: These are the amounts of sugarpaste you will need to cover one cake, if you are covering more than one then you will need less than the amounts for each cake added together, as you will be able to reuse the trimmings.

Covering a cake with sugarpaste

1 For a fruit cake, moisten the surface of the marzipan with an even coating of clear spirit, such as gin or vodka, to prevent air bubbles forming under the sugarpaste. For sponge cakes, place the cake on a hardboard cake board the same size as the cake and place on waxed paper. Cover the cake with a thin layer of buttercream to fill in any holes and help the sugarpaste stick to the surface of the cake.

2 Knead the sugarpaste until warm and pliable. Roll out on a surface lightly smeared with white vegetable fat (shortening) rather than icing (confectioners') sugar – fat works well, and you don't have the problems of icing sugar drying out or marking the sugarpaste. Roll out the paste to a depth of 5mm (³⁄₁₆in) using spacers to ensure an even thickness (**A**).

3 Lift the paste carefully over the top of the cake, supporting it with a rolling pin, and position it so that it covers the cake (**B**). Using a smoother, smooth the top surface of the cake to remove any lumps and bumps. Smooth the top edge using the palm of your hand. Always make sure your hands are clean and dry with no traces of cake crumbs before smoothing sugarpaste.

4 Using a cupped hand and an upward movement, encourage the sugarpaste on the sides of the cake to adjust to the shape of your cake (**C**). Do not press down on any pleats in the paste, instead open them out and redistribute the paste, until the cake is completely covered. Smooth the sides using a smoother.

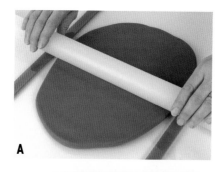

A

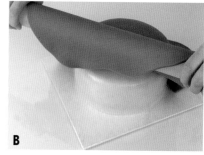

B

C

D

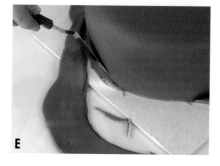

E

F

5 Take the smoother and while pressing down, run the flat edge around the base of the cake to create a cutting line (**D**). Trim away the excess paste with a palette knife (**E**) to create a neat, smooth edge (**F**).

Covering a cake to give sharp corners

Sometimes, you may wish to have sharp corners on your cake, as seen on the Stacked Hatboxes cake project on pages 22–25. To do this you will need to cover the cake with separate pieces of sugarpaste to maintain the edges. This results in a join, so think carefully if it is better to have the join on the side or the top of the cake. For the hatboxes cake the join is on the side, as it is covered by the rim of the lid, so the sides are covered first then the top.

The sides

1 Knead the sugarpaste until warm then roll into a long sausage to a length equal to the circumference of the cake. Place the sausage on your work surface and roll over to widen the paste to at least the height of the cake and thin to a thickness of 5mm (³⁄₁₆in). Cut one edge straight.

2 Cover the sides of the cake with a thin layer of buttercream. Carefully roll up the sugarpaste like a bandage then unroll it around the sides of the cake so the cut edge is flush with the lower edge of the cake. Take a smoother and smooth the paste to give it an even surface.

3 Roughly cut away the excess paste with scissors. Note: you are just removing the excess weight, not giving a neat finish.

The top

1 Roll out some more sugarpaste and use to cover the top of the cake. Roughly cut away the excess overhanging paste with a pair of scissors.

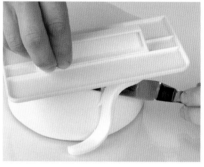

2 Place the smoother onto the surface of the sugarpaste so that it slightly overhangs the edge of the cake then using a palette knife, neatly remove the excess paste by cutting away from the cake onto the smoother.

tip...

If you have air bubbles under the icing, insert a scriber or clean glass-headed dressmakers' pin at an angle and press out the air.

4 Place the smoother onto the surface of the sugarpaste so that it partially rests above the edge of the cake then, using a palette knife, neatly remove the excess paste by cutting away from the cake onto the smoother.

Covering boards

Covering a board with sugarpaste gives you a canvas on which to add decoration to complement and enhance your cake design.

1 Roll out the sugarpaste to a thickness of 4mm (⅛in) or 5mm (³⁄₁₆in) using spacers.

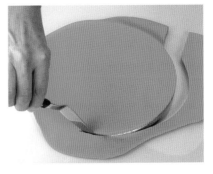

2 Moisten the board with cooled boiled water or sugar glue. Lift up the paste and drape over the board.

3 Circle a smoother over the paste to achieve a smooth, flat finish to the board.

4 Cut the paste flush with the sides of the board using a cranked handled palette knife, taking care to keep the edge vertical. The covered board should ideally be left overnight to dry thoroughly.

Using a multi-sized ribbon cutter

This tool is a great time saver as it enables you to cut strips the same size, easily and quickly.

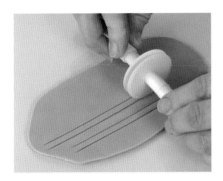

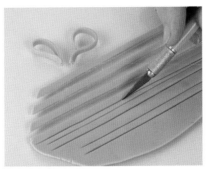

1 Assemble your tool so that the cutting wheels are set to the required width. Thinly roll out some modelling paste. Holding the handles of the tool in either hand, firmly and evenly roll the cutting edges of the tool through the paste.

2 You should be left with a beautifully cut ribbon. If the tool hasn't cut cleanly through all the paste, perhaps due to uneven pressure, run a craft knife along the edges to tidy it up. Leave the paste to firm up for a moment or two then pick it up and use as desired.

tip...
Strips cut with one straight and one wavy edge are great for trimming the join between a cake and its board.

Covering cupcakes

It is worth doing a little preparation before covering your cupcakes. Not all cupcakes come out of the oven perfect, some may need a little trimming with a sharp knife while others benefit from a little building up with an appropriate icing.

1 Check each of your cupcakes to ensure that the decoration is going to sit just as you want it to and remedy any that aren't quite right.

2 The sugarpaste may need a little help to secure it to the cupcakes, so brush the cakes with an appropriate syrup or alcohol or add a thin layer of buttercream or ganache, this also adds flavour and interest to the cakes.

3 Knead the sugarpaste until warm and pliable. Roll out on a surface lightly smeared with white vegetable fat (shortening), rather than icing (confectioners') sugar. Roll out the paste to a depth of 5mm (³⁄₁₆in). It is a good idea to use spacers for this, as they ensure an even thickness.

4 Cut out circles of sugarpaste using an appropriately sized cutter. The size of the circle required will be dependant on the cupcake pan and case used and the amount the cakes have domed.

5 Using a palette knife, carefully lift the paste circles onto each cupcake. Use the palm of your hand to shape the paste to the cupcake, easing the fullness in if necessary.

Covering cookies

Sugarpaste is an excellent and very versatile medium for cookie decoration as it allows you to be extremely creative.

1 Smear white vegetable fat (shortening) over your work surface to prevent the icing sticking. Knead the sugarpaste to warm before use.

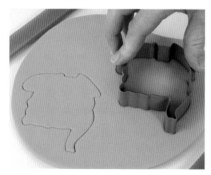

4 Carefully lift the sugarpaste shape using a palette knife to prevent distorting the shape and place on top of the cookie. If the cookie cutter has left a ragged edge around the base of the shape, just carefully tuck this under with a finger before placing on the cookie.

5 Run a finger around the top cut edge of the sugarpaste to smooth and curve it.

2 Roll out the kneaded sugarpaste to a thickness of 5mm (³⁄₁₆in) and cut out a shape using the same cookie cutter used to create the cookie. Remove the excess paste.

3 Paint piping gel over the top of the baked cookie to act as glue. Alternatively use buttercream or boiled jam.

Stacking Cakes

A multi-tiered cake, like a building, needs a structure hidden within it to prevent it from collapsing. It is important that this structure is 'built' correctly to take the loads put upon it, so follow these instructions carefully, as it is worth the time involved to get this stage correct.

Dowelling the cakes

All but the top tier will usually need dowelling to provide support.

1 Place the cakes to be stacked on hardboard cake boards of the same size as the cakes and cover each cake with sugarpaste, this ensures the boards are not visible yet gives the stacked cakes stability.

2 To support the cakes, dowels need to be inserted into all but the top tier. To do this, take the base cake and place a cake board the same size as the tier above in the centre of the cake. Scribe around the edge of the board to leave a visible outline.

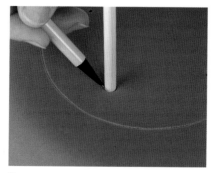

3 Insert a dowel 2.5cm (1in) in from the scribed line vertically down through the cake to the cake board below. Make a knife scratch or pencil mark on the dowel to mark the exact height and remove the dowel.

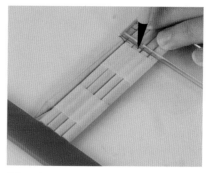

4 Tape four dowels together. Then, using the mark on the inserted dowel, draw a pencil cutting line over the tape on the four dowels, making sure that the line is 90 degrees to the dowels (a set square helps). Next, using a small saw, such as a mitre saw that holds the dowels firm as it cuts, saw across the dowels.

5 Place one of the dowels back in the measuring hole and insert the other dowels vertically down to the cake board at 3, 6 and 9 o'clock to the first one.

6 Repeat steps 1–5 for all but the top cake. It is essential that all the dowels are inserted vertically, are all the same length and have flat tops.

Stacking the cakes

Cover and dowel each cake before stacking. Place 15ml (1 tbsp) royal icing within the scribed area of the base cake and stack the next sized cake on top using the scribed line as a placement guide. Repeat the process with the remaining cakes.

Suppliers

Lindy's Cakes Ltd (LC)

Unit 2, Station Approach, Wendover
Buckinghamshire HP22 6BN
Tel: +44 (0)1296 622418
www.lindyscakes.co.uk
Online shop for products and
equipment used in this and Lindy's
other books, including Lindy's own
ranges of cutters and stencils

Abbreviations used in this booklet

DS – Designer Stencils

FI – First Impressions

FMM – FMM Sugarcraft

LC – Lindy's Cakes Ltd

PME – PME Sugarcraft

SF – Sugarflair

SK – Squires Kitchen

W – Wilton

UK

Alan Silverwood Ltd
Ledsam House, Ledsam Street
Birmingham B16 8DN
Tel: +44 (0)121 454 3571
www.alansilverwood.co.uk
Manufacturer of multi-sized cake
pan, multi mini cake pans and
spherical moulds/ball tins

Ceefor Cakes
PO Box 443, Leighton Buzzard
Bedforshire LU7 1AJ
Tel: +44 (0)1525 375237
www.ceeforcakes.co.uk
Supplier of strong cake boxes –
most sizes available

FMM Sugarcraft (FMM)
Unit 7, Chancerygate Business
Park, Whiteleaf Road,
Hemel Hempstead, Hertfordshire
HP3 9HD
Tel: +44 (0)1442 292970
www.fmmsugarcraft.com
Manufacturer of cutters

Holly Products (HP)
Primrose Cottage, Church Walk,
Norton in Hales
Shropshire, TF9 4QX
Tel: +44 (0)1630 655759
www.hollyproducts.co.uk
Manufacturer and supplier of
embossing sticks and moulds

M&B Specialised Confectioners Ltd
3a Millmead Estate, Mill Mead
Road
London N17 9ND
Tel: +44 (0)208 801 7948
www.mbsc.co.uk
Manufacturer and supplier of
sugarpaste

Patchwork Cutters (PC)
Unit 12, Arrowe Commercial Park,
Arrowe Brook Road, Upton
Wirral CH49 1AB
Tel: +44 (0)151 678 5053
www.patchworkcutters.co.uk
Manufacturer and supplier of
cutters and embossers

US

Global Sugar Art
625 Route 3, Unit 3
Plattsburgh, NY 12901
Tel: 1-518-561-3039 or 1-800-420-6088
(toll free)
www.globalsugarart.com
Sugarcraft supplier that imports many UK
products to the US

Cake Craft Shoppe
3530 Highway 6
Sugar Land, TX 77478
Tel: 1-281-491-3920
www.cakecraftshoppe.com
Sugarcraft supplier

First Impressions Molds
300 Business Park Way, Suite A-200
Royal Palm Beach, FL 33411
Tel: 1-561-784-7186
www.firstimpressionsmolds.com
Manufacturer and supplier of moulds

Australia

Iced Affair
53 Church Street
Camperdown NSW 2050
Tel: +61 (0)2 9519 3679
www.icedaffair.com.au
Sugarcraft supplier